POINT OF IMPACT

The Fall of the Berlin Wall

The Cold War Ends

NIGEL KELLY

Heinemann Library
Chicago, Illinois

© 2001 Reed Educational & Professional Publishing
Published by Heinemann Library,
an imprint of Reed Educational & Professional Publishing,
100 N. LaSalle, Suite 1010
Chicago, IL 60602
Customer Service 888-454-2279
Visit our website at www.heinemannlibrary.com

Design and map artwork by Robert Sydenham, Ambassador Design Ltd, Bristol.
Originated by Ambassador Litho, Bristol.
Printed in Hong Kong

05 04 03 02 01
10 9 8 7 6 5 4 3 2 1

Library of Congress Cataloging-in-Publication Data
Kelly, Nigel.
    The fall of the Berlin Wall : the Cold War ends / Nigel Kelly.
        p. cm. – (Point of impact)
    Includes bibliographical references and index.
    Summary: Using the Berlin Wall as the focus, traces the history of the Cold War, from the Russian Revolution in 1917 through World War II, and finally to the destruction of the Wall..
    ISBN 1-57572-413-8 (library binding)
    1. Berlin Wall, Berlin, Germany, 1961-1989—Juvenile literature. 2. Berlin (Germany)—Politics and government—1945-1990—Juvenile literature. [1. Cold War. 2. Berlin Wall, Berlin, Germany, 1961-1989. 3. Berlin (Germany)—Politics and government—1945-1990.] I. Title. II. Series.

DD881 .K38 2001
943'.155087—dc21
                         00-024333

Acknowledgments
The Publishers would like to thank the following for permission to reproduce photographs: Bridgeman, p. 6; Centre for the Study of Cartoon and Caricature, pp. 10, 18; Corbis, p. 4 (AFP), pp. 16, 17 (Bettman), pp. 23, 25; Hulton Getty, pp. 8, 15; David King, pp. 7, 11; Magnum Photos, p. 21 (Joseph Koudelka); Rex Features, p. 20; Shone/Gamma/Frank Spooner pictures, p. 28; Sipa Press, p. 24.

Cover photograph reproduced with permission of Corbis.

Our thanks to Christopher Gibb for his help in the preparation of this book.

Every effort has been made to contact copyright holders of any material reproduced in this book. Any omissions will be rectified in subsequent printings if notice is given to the Publisher.

Some words are shown in bold, **like this.** You can find out what they mean by looking in the glossary.

Contents

The Wall Comes Down

Knocking down the wall

On November 9, 1989, people all over Germany celebrated the decision to knock down a wall. Thousands of them even went to Berlin to help knock it down. However, it was not just any wall—it was the most hated boundary in history. This concrete barrier, 16 feet (5 meters) high, was a symbol of the division between two different political beliefs and two different ways of life. The **Berlin Wall** did not just divide East and West Berlin. It was also the division between the **communist** governments of Eastern Europe and the **democracies** of Western Europe and the U.S.—known as the West.

The people of Berlin hated the wall because its creation had split families and friends and divided their city in two. But what made the people so happy that night in 1989 was that they saw the breaching of the wall as a sign of a much more important event in international relations. For more than 40 years, the countries of Eastern Europe and those of the West, led by the United States, had been involved in a **Cold War.**

Here, the hated Berlin Wall begins to fall. Just a few days before this, anyone attacking the wall would have been shot dead!

The Cold War

The Cold War was not a military war. Instead, it was a war of words where the two sides, East and West, tried to extend their influence and score victories. They used **propaganda** to emphasize their own good points or to discredit their opponents. Many people feared that the world was constantly on the brink of a real war.

CAPITALISM

Wealthy people (capitalists) invest their money in land and industry. They employ workers and keep all the profits that are made. A democratic system is followed, with a number of political parties.

COMMUNISM

There is a classless society. There is no individual profit-making, and land and industry are owned by the state. Profits are used for the good of all. There is only one political party.

During the Cold War, both East and West poured huge sums of money into researching and developing more and more advanced weapons. Each side wanted to have greater military power than the other. Among their weapons were atomic bombs, which had first been used by the United States on Hiroshima, Japan, leading to the end of World War II in 1945. Such weapons led to a fear that the Cold War might turn "hot," resulting in wide-scale destruction and millions of deaths.

What the people of Berlin were hoping was that if the very symbol of this Cold War—the Berlin Wall—came down, then surely the Cold War itself would soon end. East and West might be able to live in peace and cooperate. If this proved to be the case, the fall of the Berlin Wall would truly be a turning point in world history.

Communism and **capitalism** are very different ideas.

INTO A NEW WORLD

"Even though it is the middle of the night, we woke up the children and brought them to the wall for this historic occasion. It is important that they see the tremendous things that are happening here. . . ."
These were the words spoken by a 41-year-old man living in East Berlin on November 9, 1989. As he spoke, hundreds of young East and West Berliners were climbing to the top of the wall to greet each other. Many of them used chisels and hammers to chip away souvenirs of the historic night.

How It All Began

The Russian Revolution

The **Cold War** actually had its origins in 1917. In that year, the last **czar** of Russia was overthrown and eventually replaced by a **Bolshevik**—later renamed **communist**—government. The name of the country, Russia, was changed to the **Soviet Union.**

The governments of the West did not approve of the new communist system and wanted to destroy it. They sent troops to Russia to help forces fighting against the communists in a bitter **civil war.** The communists won and became the undisputed rulers of Russia. However, the communist leaders did not trust the West, and were convinced that if any chance arose to destroy **communism,** the West would take it.

Distrust

In the West, the **capitalist** countries were just as suspicious. They thought that the Soviet Union wanted to spread communism worldwide by overthrowing the existing governments of other countries and replacing them with communist ones. The Western countries were just as distrustful of the Soviet Union as it was of them.

In November 1917, Bolshevik troops stormed the Winter Palace, which was the headquarters of the regional government, and seized power.

Adolf Hitler

In the 1930s, there was a chance for the two sides to put their differences aside and become friends. Both groups were very concerned when, in 1933, Adolf Hitler became the new German leader. He was promising the German people to make Germany strong and win back what it had lost in World War I (1914–18).

The Soviet Union was worried because Hitler hated communism and wanted to gain Soviet lands. The West was worried, too. The U.S. was trying not to be drawn into other countries' affairs. Both Britain and France knew that if Germany became strong again, it might want to fight another war. To try to avoid this, they had a policy of **appeasement** toward Germany. This meant that they gave in to Hitler's demands as long as these did not seem too unreasonable. They were determined not to repeat the death and destruction of World War I. The Soviets thought that the West was being friendly with Hitler in the hope that he would attack the Soviet Union. If he did, Germany and the Soviet Union would both become weaker, which would please the West.

This Soviet cartoon is from the 1930s. It is criticizing Britain and France, whose leaders are shown directing Hitler and his generals away from the West and toward the Soviet Union. The Soviets thought that Britain and France were being friendly to Hitler so that he would destroy the Soviet Union.

The best thing would have been for the West and the Soviet Union to join together as **allies** after 1933, but they did not trust each other enough for that. In the end, there was an astonishing agreement made in 1939 between the Soviet Union and Germany, called the Nazi–Soviet Pact. The two countries hated each other, but for the moment it was to their advantage to be allies.

Deteriorating Relations

Despite the policy of **appeasement,** World War II broke out in Europe in September 1939. Within two years, the **Soviet Union** and Germany were at war.

Now that they were all fighting **Nazi** Germany, Britain, the United States, France, and the Soviet Union became **allies.** But even when they were fighting on the same side, the West and the Soviet Union were still suspicious of each other. The Western countries were determined to make sure that the Soviet Union did not become more powerful after the war. This was to prove very difficult.

The Germans had invaded the Soviet Union in 1941, but by 1945, they had been defeated. Soviet troops were slowly advancing across Europe until they met British, French, and American troops in Berlin. At that point, the Germans surrendered, and the war in Europe was over.

Soviet troops and American troops met in Berlin in April 1945. For the moment, they were great friends, but the friendship did not last.

The Soviet empire

As the Soviet army advanced across Europe, it liberated, or freed, many countries from Nazi rule. These countries, including Hungary and Czechoslovakia, were grateful to the Soviet Union, and many people were happy to elect **communists** to govern them. However, sometimes the Soviet leader, Joseph Stalin, used force to make sure that countries cooperated. Soon, communist governments loyal to the Soviet Union had been set up across Eastern Europe. The Soviet Union had also taken the opportunity to move its own border 300 miles (480 kilometers) west by taking over territory in Latvia, Lithuania, Estonia, and Poland.

The fears of the West

The Soviet Union thought that it was protecting itself by setting up friendly communist governments in Eastern Europe. The Western countries, however—particularly the U.S.—saw Stalin's progress as the first step toward spreading **communism** through Europe and across the world.

Winston Churchill, who had been prime minister of Britain during the war, spoke of an **"Iron Curtain"** being drawn across Europe by Stalin. This name soon stuck, as a 1,000-mile (1,600-kilometer) series of fences, protected by razor wire, dog runs, guard towers, and remote-controlled weapons, was erected to separate Eastern and Western Europe.

The U.S. decided to take steps to stop this "communist advance." In March 1947, President Harry Truman said that his country would help any government threatened either from within or from outside its own borders. This policy was the **Truman Doctrine.** In June 1947, Truman announced the **Marshall Plan,** offering huge grants of American money to help European countries recover from the war. Stalin banned the countries of Eastern Europe from applying for these grants. The friendly relations that had grown during World War II were soon long gone.

Territory gained by USSR in 1945

Countries under communist control

Communist but independent

Iron Curtain

After World War II, Europe was divided by the Iron Curtain.

THE IRON CURTAIN

"From Stettin in the Baltic to Trieste in the Adriatic, an iron curtain has descended across the continent. . . . The growth of communist parties in these countries poses a growing challenge to Christian civilization." Winston Churchill spoke these words to an American audience in March 1946. He was very suspicious of Soviet actions, but since the war had only just ended, not everyone shared his anxieties. Some Americans felt that Churchill was being too tough on the Soviet Union.

Communism versus Capitalism

Superpower rivalry

The distrust that East and West had for each other, and the division of Europe by the **Iron Curtain,** resulted in more than 40 years of bitter rivalry that became known as the **Cold War.** The leading players in this rivalry were the United States and the **Soviet Union.** These two countries were so large and powerful that historians often refer to them as **superpowers.**

The Soviet Union dominated Eastern Europe and made sure that the **communist** governments in countries behind the Iron Curtain were loyal to its leadership. The United States did not control Western Europe in the same way, but as the world's richest country, it had great influence, and was generally accepted as the leader of the West by countries such as France and Britain.

This American cartoon shows "Uncle Sam," who represents the U.S., being asked to help Western Europe. It is clearly in his interests to do so!

"Come on, Sam! It's up to us again"

Containing communism

During this period, one of the major aims of the United States was to prevent the further spread of **communism.** The Americans called this policy "containment"—the **Marshall Plan** was part of this policy. The U.S. believed that when people were unhappy, beliefs like communism could sound very attractive. Unhappiness is often caused by poverty, and there was plenty of poverty in Europe after the war. Germany, for example, had suffered heavy bombing that had reduced some of its major cities almost to rubble. Between 1948 and 1952, the United States provided over $13 billion to help European countries fight poverty and recover from problems created by the war.

This Soviet painting shows the Soviet leader, Stalin, meeting industrial workers. In the picture, they all look very happy, but the true situation was very different.

Different views

It is interesting to note that in 1947, a leading Soviet official described the Marshall Plan as "an American plan to enslave Europe." It is clear that the two sides saw things differently, and that there was much distrust and misunderstanding during the Cold War.

Of course, the Soviet Union was also issuing **propaganda.** One effective way it did this was by showing how popular communism was in the Soviet Union. The painting above gives a very positive impression of workers' relationship with their leader, Stalin. Who would guess from this that workers complained bitterly about long hours and low pay in the Soviet Union? Or that Stalin sent an estimated twenty million people to **labor camps,** where over half of them died?

THE MARSHALL PLAN— OPPOSING VIEWS

The cartoon opposite shows how many Americans saw the Marshall Plan. It suggests that Uncle Sam, who represents the U.S., is going to have to rescue Western Europe again. The cartoon is a piece of propaganda. That means that it is exaggerating the truth to get a point across.

Notice how the American's garden looks very neat and tidy, and how Western Europe's house is going to fall down without American help. The message of the cartoon is that the U.S. is a kind and helpful country that runs its affairs well and will help Europe. But the cartoon also has a message for the American people. If the house falls down, it will fall on the American house. The cartoonist clearly thought that if Western Europe became communist, the United States would be under threat, too.

The Berlin Blockade

After World War II, Germany was divided into four zones, each governed by one of the four main **allies** in the war—Britain, the U.S., France, and the **Soviet Union.** By 1948, Britain, France, and the United States had decided to join their areas together and introduce a new currency to try to make the unified area more prosperous. Stalin was worried, because this plan would make the Soviet zone look poor in comparison. He did not have the money to build it up to the same level as the Western zones. He also objected to the other three allies having any control of Berlin, because the city was in the part of Germany controlled by the Soviet Union.

Germany and its capital, Berlin, were divided after World War II. Each of the four victorious forces (the U.S., Britain, France, and the Soviet Union) took control of an area of Berlin.

On June 24, 1948, he decided to try to force the three Western countries to give up their zones. He set up a **blockade** by cutting all road, rail, and water links between the British, French, and American parts of Germany and their zones in Berlin (now called West Berlin). He knew that West Berlin had enough food and fuel for only six weeks, and he expected the three Western allies to let the Soviet Union take control of their zones. As far as he could see, their only alternative was to use tanks to smash through the road and rail blocks and bring in supplies. Such an aggressive action was bound to cause war, and he doubted they would do that.

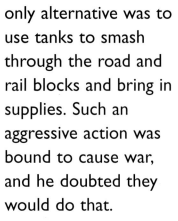

N

EAST GERMANY

WEST GERMANY

POLAND

Soviet Checkpoint

Checkpoint Charlie

Brandenburg Gate

WEST BERLIN

EAST BERLIN

British occupied zone
US occupied zone
French occupied zone
USSR occupied zone

0 km   500 km

0 mi   300 mi

The Berlin airlift

Stalin had not counted on the West's determination to keep West Berlin. They decided to fly supplies into the city. If Stalin wanted to stop the supplies, he would have to shoot the planes down. What would people think of a leader who shot down planes carrying food and fuel to people in need? To help persuade Stalin that shooting down the planes would be an unwise move, the Americans stationed B-29 bombers in Britain—ready to drop atomic bombs on the Soviet Union if necessary.

Over the next eleven months, the three Western allies made 277,728 air trips from their bases in Germany into West Berlin. They delivered over two million tons of supplies. Eventually, Stalin had to accept that the West was committed to keeping West Berlin, and he called off his blockade.

PRESIDENT CLINTON

In 1998, U.S. President Bill Clinton visited Berlin to celebrate the fiftieth anniversary of the Berlin blockade and airlift. In his speech, he called Berlin "the first battlefield of the **Cold War**." At the time, no one really thought that it was possible to supply a city from the air, but a few forward-thinking people were convinced it could be done.

LITTLE TREATS—CANDY PARACHUTES

During the airlift, a U.S. pilot named Gail S. Halvorsen began making small parachutes out of scraps of cloth. He used them to drop candy to children in West Berlin. As news of his action spread, donations of thousands of dollars worth of sweets and scrap cloth came in from across the United States. By January 1949, more than 250,000 "candy parachutes" had been dropped to the excited and grateful children of West Berlin.

This postcard was sent by a grateful child in West Berlin. The message reads, *"130 days airlift. We thank the pilots for their work and effort."*

Building the Wall

Stalin had hoped that people living in East Berlin and the Soviet-controlled zone of Germany—known as East Germany as of 1949—would not feel that West Berlin was a more attractive place to live. But the money that the Western **allies** put into building up their zones made West Germany more prosperous, with higher wages and a higher standard of living. From May 1949 to 1961, an estimated two and a half million people left East Germany to live and work in the West. Many of them were skilled engineers and professional people whose talents were sorely missed in the East. In 1960, for example, 688 doctors, 296 dentists, and 2,648 engineers crossed over.

Stopping the flow

In June 1961, Stalin's successor, Nikita Khrushchev, demanded that the Western powers leave Berlin. U.S. President John F. Kennedy flew to West Berlin to assure the people living there that he would not allow them to fall under **communist** control. The people were delighted to hear him say, *"Ich bin ein Berliner"* (I am a Berliner)—although in German, a "Berliner" is actually a kind of doughnut!

Khrushchev decided that if the Western allies would not leave West Berlin, he would cut all contact between the two halves of the city. It was already virtually impossible for people "behind the **Iron Curtain**" to cross to the West—except from East Berlin to West Berlin.

This shows the number of East Germans crossing into West Germany between 1949–62. Notice the sharp drop in numbers after the **Berlin Wall** was built in 1961.

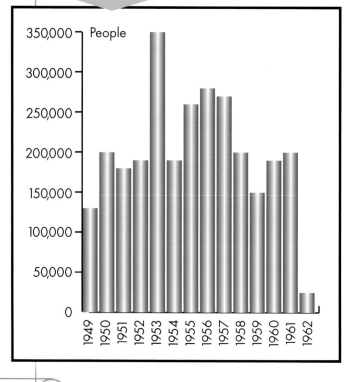

The Berlin Wall divided East Berlin from West Berlin.

Plugging the gap

Now it was time to mend "the hole" in the Iron Curtain, through which so many of East Germany's skilled people were leaving.

On August 13, 1961, the East German government erected a border of barbed wire and soldiers armed with machine guns between East and West Berlin. Three days later, work started on a 30-mile (45-kilometer) concrete wall. It was announced that anyone trying to cross the wall would be shot.

THE MEMORIES OF MARGIT HOSSEINI

Margit Hosseini lived in West Berlin when the wall was built. In 1996, she gave an interview that provided many useful insights into what life was like in the city.

Life before the wall was built

"The main difference between East Berlin and West Berlin showed in clothes. If we ever visited East Berlin, we always took clothes, because ours were much nicer. We also took oranges, because oranges were unobtainable in East Berlin."

An incident at the wall

"I was staying with friends near the wall and we heard something was happening. We went to look. There was a wounded man lying in the border zone. At first he screamed, he cried, he shouted for help. And as the hours went on, his voice got weaker, until he stopped. I felt it was so heartrending that in the middle of nowhere was a human being dying, and the two groups were facing each other too worried to act. I was just crying—it was really horrible. I am sure the soldiers felt the same, on both sides."

This incident was probably the failed attempt to cross the wall, described on page 17.

Crossing the Wall

At first, there were some problems for the East German authorities trying to keep people from crossing the **Berlin Wall.** In places, the wall ran past buildings, which became part of the dividing line between East and West Berlin. In the first few weeks after the building of the wall, some East Germans jumped from windows in these buildings to be caught by the crowd below. One 59-year-old woman threw a mattress out of an upper-floor window and jumped into West Berlin. She died of her injuries.

The West Berlin fire department began sending firemen with blankets to catch people jumping from upper-floor windows. In one famous case, a woman tried to jump out of a window, but was held back by East German police as West German firemen waited below to catch her. She eventually managed to break free, and was caught safely by the firemen.

A German woman is being lowered from East Berlin to West.

Failed attempts

Although there were many spectacular escapes, the windows of buildings on the border were soon bricked up, and machine-gun posts, guards, and minefields prevented safe crossings. Forty-one East Germans lost their lives crossing the wall in its first year. Among them was a young man named Peter Fechter.

The body of Peter Fechter lies in Soviet-controlled territory, close to the Berlin Wall. He almost made it to the West.

PETER FECHTER

Peter Fechter was an eighteen-year-old bricklayer from East Berlin. In 1962, he decided to cross the Berlin Wall to be with his sister, Hilfe, in West Berlin. Together with a friend, he dashed across a border of sand and began scaling the wall. His friend managed to get over the barbed wire on top of the wall, but Fechter hesitated and was shot in the back by the border police. He fell back to the ground and lay bleeding to death. He could be heard crying pitifully for help.

Just 1,000 feet (300 meters) away was a U.S. command post, Checkpoint Charlie. Crowds on the West Berlin side begged the Americans to rescue the boy, but the soldiers on patrol were ordered not to intervene. Fechter was in Soviet-controlled territory, and any intervention might cause an international incident. More than fifty minutes after he had been shot, his body was taken away by East Berlin guards. He was one of many East Germans to die trying to cross the wall.

The Cuban Missile Crisis

Part of the **Cold War** was a deadly contest to have more and better weapons than the other side. By 1962, the **Soviet Union** and the United States had built up huge stockpiles of nuclear weapons, and could even fire missiles from nuclear submarines under the sea. Each of the **superpowers** had nuclear missile bases, although the U.S. had the advantage of being more or less out of range of Soviet missiles.

This cartoon from a British newspaper shows leaders Kennedy, Khrushchev, and Castro as gunslingers from the old American West. The cartoonist is suggesting that the Cuban missile crisis was really a personal contest of strength among them.

On the brink of war

Cuba is an island just 90 miles (150 kilometers) off the coast of the U.S. In 1959, Fidel Castro, who was friendly with the Soviet Union, became Cuba's leader. In April 1961, U.S. President Kennedy supported an attempt to overthrow Castro, but it was easily defeated, and the Americans were made to look foolish. More significantly, Castro was angered and became even friendlier with the Soviet Union.

The missile threat

In October 1962, American spy planes found evidence of sites for nuclear missiles on Cuba. News also reached Kennedy that a Soviet fleet was heading for Cuba, probably carrying missiles. If missile bases were successfully established on Cuba, so close to the U.S., virtually the whole of the United States would be threatened. Kennedy would not allow this to happen.

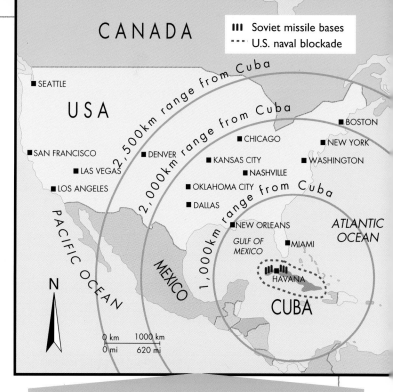

This map shows the potential range of Soviet nuclear weapons fired from Cuba. Almost all of the U.S. was in danger!

Crisis time

Kennedy decided to put a **blockade** around Cuba and not let any ships through. He also called on Khrushchev to remove the missiles already in Cuba. Khrushchev refused. He said that the West had missiles stationed in countries all around the Soviet Union, such as Iran and Turkey, so they had no right to object to what he was doing. As the ships sailed closer to Cuba, the world waited. If the U.S. sank the Soviet ships, war was almost inevitable.

Khrushchev was really trying to see just how far the U.S. president was prepared to go, and finally ordered the ships to turn around. The Soviets then agreed to remove the missiles already installed on Cuba, in return for a promise from the United States not to invade the island. The crisis was over and war had been avoided, but it had been close. To try to prevent future misunderstandings, a direct **hot line** telephone link was set up between the U.S. capital, Washington, D.C., and the Soviet capital, Moscow.

DISCREDITING CASTRO

In 1962, American military chiefs began thinking of ways they could discredit Fidel Castro. Among the suggestions were:

● Sink a boatload of refugees crossing from Cuba to the U.S. and blame it on Castro.

● Be prepared to blame Castro if the 1962 space flight carrying John Glenn crashed.

● Prepare a poisoned scuba-diving suit as a gift for Castro.

● Blow up an American warship and blame it on Castro.

Fortunately, none of these ideas were carried out.

Hungary and Czechoslovakia

Although the **Soviet Union** ruled other **communist** Eastern European countries very strictly, there were still times when Soviet military strength was needed to keep some of them in line. Two such examples were in Hungary and Czechoslovakia.

The Hungarian rebellion

When Stalin died in 1953, Khrushchev, his successor, had criticized him for not letting the people of Eastern Europe have more freedom. The Hungarian people hoped this meant they could have **freedom of speech** and the right to follow their Catholic Christian religion.

In 1956, the Hungarian prime minister, Imre Nagy, announced that Hungary would leave the Warsaw Pact. This Pact was an alliance of all the communist countries in Eastern Europe. It had been set up in 1955 in opposition to the North Atlantic Treaty Organization (NATO), a military organization formed by the Western powers in 1949.

Soviet tanks drove through the streets of Budapest, the capital of Hungary, during the crushing of the Hungarian rebellion.

Khrushchev feared that if Hungary left the Warsaw Pact, other communist countries might do the same, so on November 4, 1956, he sent 200,000 troops into Hungary. Many Hungarians took up arms to defend their country, but Hungary was soon back under Soviet control. Thousands of Hungarians died in the rebellion, and Nagy was taken to Moscow and executed.

A drawing on a wall of a Prague street in 1968 showed that in 1945, the Soviet army had been welcomed because it freed Czechoslovakia from German rule. But in 1968, the army returned as attackers.

The Prague Spring

In 1968, the Czech leader, Alexander Dubček, began to make changes in Czechoslovakia to give people more freedom. He permitted foreign travel, ended **censorship,** and allowed public meetings and discussions. People described his changes as the "Prague Spring" because there was a thaw from the old harsh way of life. Dubček reassured the Soviet leader, Leonid Brezhnev (who had taken over from Khrushchev in 1964), that Czechoslovakia had no intention of leaving the Warsaw Pact and that the changes were no threat to the Soviet Union.

However, Brezhnev was not convinced. On August 20, 1968, Soviet troops invaded Czechoslovakia. The Soviet soldiers had been told that they were there at the invitation of the Czech government to put down troublemakers. They could not understand why the Czech people jeered and spat at them. Dubček was arrested and dismissed. Soviet authority was restored, and the changes Dubček had made were reversed.

A PLEA FROM A HUNGARIAN RADIO STATION

*"Civilized people of the world, listen and come to our aid with soldiers and arms. Do not forget that there is no stopping the wild attack of **communism.** Your turn will come, once we perish."*

When this broadcast was made in November 1956, Soviet troops were advancing into Hungary. Despite the pleas for help, the West did nothing to stop the Russian invasion.

The Vietnam War

The **Soviet Union** had chosen not to provoke war over the Cuban missile crisis, but later in the 1960s, the Americans and Soviets came close to direct fighting over Vietnam, in Asia.

A divided country

Vietnam was divided into two countries. North Vietnam was a **communist** country, receiving money and support from the Soviet Union. South Vietnam was an anticommunist country. Its government, however, was having trouble with communist **guerrillas** in its territory. The guerrillas, known as the Vietcong, were receiving support from North Vietnam and the Soviet Union. They wanted to overthrow the South Vietnamese government and set up a communist government in its place.

The Americans were concerned that if South Vietnam became communist, then the countries surrounding it would fall one by one—like dominoes knocking each other over. They called this concept the "Domino Theory."

The Domino Theory stated that if one country falls to communism, it takes the rest with it.

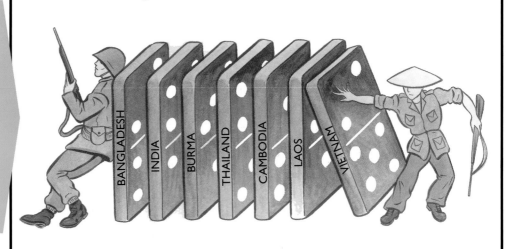

22

Many U.S. troops saw action in the Vietnam War.

War begins and ends

Beginning in 1954, the United States sent experts to help train the South Vietnamese army and fight against the Vietcong. The U.S. said these people were "advisers," but really, many of them were military officers and soldiers. Despite this American help, the South Vietnamese could not defeat the Vietcong, so the U.S. sent more troops. By 1965, there were over 180,000 U.S. troops in Vietnam, but they found it very difficult to defeat an army skilled in jungle warfare. By 1968, the American public no longer wanted to tolerate the cost of the war, or the terrible attacks on innocent villagers that were sometimes carried out by frustrated American soldiers.

In 1973, U.S. President Richard Nixon helped negotiate a cease-fire, and United States troops left Vietnam. The war had cost 58,000 U.S. lives and over a million Vietnamese. By 1976, North Vietnamese forces had overrun South Vietnam and joined the two countries together as one communist country.

A NUCLEAR DETERRENT?

It was interesting to note that the Americans had many nuclear weapons, but they chose not to use them in Vietnam—even though they could not win the war otherwise. Despite having huge numbers of weapons, the U.S. and the Soviet Union were careful not to use them against each other. The real purpose of having nuclear weapons was to make enemy countries afraid to attack. This was called the nuclear deterrent.

Unfreezing the Cold War

The arms race

During the **Cold War,** both sides raced to create a supply of weapons superior to that of their opponent. This became known as the "arms race." This approach not only threatened world peace, but was also extremely expensive. Many schools and hospitals could be built for the price of a nuclear submarine!

It is not surprising, therefore, that during the Cold War there were occasions when the leaders of the **Soviet Union** and the U.S. tried to reach agreements to limit spending on arms and reduce tension between the two sides. They distrusted each other so much, however, that this proved very difficult.

Détente

During the Cuban missile crisis, President Kennedy suggested to the Soviet Union that they should aim to have détente, a lessening of the tension between the two sides. The setting up of the **hot line** after the Cuban missile crisis was the first step towards this. However, starting in 1965, relations between the U.S. and the Soviet Union actually became worse as they argued over Vietnam and Czechoslovakia.

This British athlete, Alan Wells, won the gold medal in the 100-meter dash at the 1980 Moscow Olympics. Some experts argue that he was able to win this medal only because the United States did not send a team to Moscow, following the Soviet Union's invasion of Afghanistan.

Breakthrough

A major breakthrough came in 1972, when the two sides signed an agreement at the end of the Strategic Arms Limitation Talks (SALT). It said that they would limit the number of nuclear missiles they were producing. In 1975, the U.S. and Soviet Union both signed the Helsinki Accords on **human rights,** and in 1979, there was another agreement about limiting arms (SALT-2). Then, on Christmas Day, 1979, the Soviet Union invaded Afghanistan. Good relations between the U.S. and the Soviet Union broke down, SALT-2 was abandoned, and the Americans refused to attend the 1980 Olympic Games, held in Moscow.

Reagan and Gorbachev

It took a change of leadership in both countries to bring about a genuine improvement in relations. In 1981, Ronald Reagan took office as U.S. president, and in 1985, Mikhail Gorbachev became the Soviet leader. Gorbachev knew that the Soviet Union was bankrupt, and he wanted to reduce spending on defense. Reagan was very suspicious of the Soviets, but many of his advisers wanted a more peaceful relationship with the Soviet Union. Reagan was also eager to cut taxation in the U.S., and saw arms reduction as a way of doing this.

Gorbachev (left) and Reagan met on friendly terms in Geneva in November 1985.

In November 1985, the two leaders met in Geneva, Switzerland, and immediately established good relations. They soon agreed to reduce nuclear missiles in Europe, and began discussions on reducing non-nuclear weapons as well. However, before any agreement could be reached on non-nuclear weapons, astonishing changes occurred in Europe.

The End of the Cold War

Glasnost and perestroika

Although Mikhail Gorbachev was very successful in bringing about improved relations with the West, he was less successful at home. He followed two main policies. *Perestroika* was the reshaping of the Soviet economy to allow more profit making by individuals and to reduce control by the government. *Glasnost* meant more openness about government and more **freedom of speech.** Criticism of government policy would be allowed, and corruption among government officials would end.

These events of 1989–90 helped lead to the end of **communist** rule in Europe.

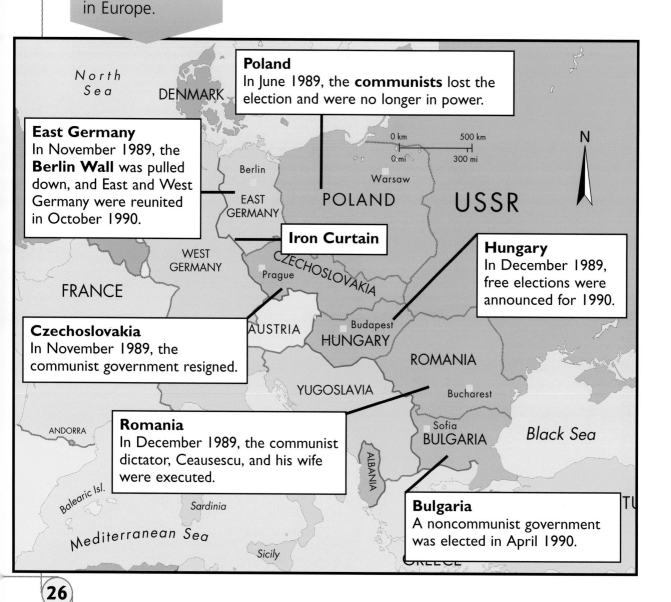

Poland
In June 1989, the **communists** lost the election and were no longer in power.

East Germany
In November 1989, the **Berlin Wall** was pulled down, and East and West Germany were reunited in October 1990.

Iron Curtain

Hungary
In December 1989, free elections were announced for 1990.

Czechoslovakia
In November 1989, the communist government resigned.

Romania
In December 1989, the communist dictator, Ceausescu, and his wife were executed.

Bulgaria
A noncommunist government was elected in April 1990.

North Sea
DENMARK
Berlin
Warsaw
0 km   500 km
0 mi   300 mi
N
EAST GERMANY
POLAND
USSR
WEST GERMANY
CZECHOSLOVAKIA
Prague
FRANCE
AUSTRIA
Budapest
HUNGARY
ROMANIA
YUGOSLAVIA
Bucharest
ANDORRA
Sofia
BULGARIA
Black Sea
ALBANIA
Balearic Isl.
Sardinia
Mediterranean Sea
Sicily
GREECE
TU

Gorbachev's policies horrified traditional Soviet communists, but at the same time led the people of the **Soviet Union** to expect greater changes than they were prepared to handle. Soon, the country was in turmoil, as people from all sides criticized the Soviet leader.

The fall of the Soviet empire

The weakening of government control was soon noticed by opponents of communism in Europe. The days when opposition to communism would mean Soviet tanks being sent in to deal with "troublemakers" were long past. Suddenly, the people of Eastern Europe realized that they no longer had anything to fear from the Soviet Union. Between May 1989 and May 1990, communist governments were overthrown in Hungary, East Germany, Bulgaria, Romania, Poland, and Czechoslovakia. The Iron Curtain had dissolved. In November 1989, the Berlin Wall was pulled down and, just one year later, East and West Germany were reunited.

In December 1989, Gorbachev and George Bush, the new U.S. president, announced that the **Cold War** was over. Gorbachev was awarded the **Nobel Peace Prize** in 1990.

THE END OF THE WALL

"What was my reaction the other night? I tell you. I'm a hard old retired colonel, but I had tears in my eyes. To see people standing on the wall, where once they would have been shot. I could hardly take it all in." These comments were made by U.S. pilot Gail S. Halvorsen after the fall of the Berlin Wall. Halvorsen was called the "Berlin Candy bomber" because of his work during the Berlin airlift.

From Cold War to Chaos

Pressure for change

By December 1989, the **Cold War** was over, the **Berlin Wall** was being dismantled, and a new era had begun in international affairs. There were dramatic changes in the **Soviet Union,** too. The country was a union of fifteen different republics, dominated by Russia and governed from the Russian capital, Moscow. Now the individual member republics of the Soviet Union began calling for more influence and a reduction in the power of Russia.

The Soviet people were also becoming increasingly unhappy with **communist** rule. In February 1990, 250,000 people demonstrated against **communism** in Moscow. Three months later, at the annual May Day parade in Red Square, Moscow, Gorbachev was heckled by demonstrators.

Gorbachev, confronted by Yeltsin in the Russian parliament, was forced to read out documents that showed it had been his own communist colleagues who had tried to overthrow him.

The fall of Gorbachev

Finally, in August 1991, there was an attempted **coup** against the Russian leader. After that, the real power lay in the hands of the mayor of Moscow, Boris Yeltsin. Gorbachev was jeered in the Russian parliament, and on August 24, 1991, he resigned as leader of the Soviet Communist party. Five days later, the Communist party officially disbanded. Then, in December 1991, the Soviet Union was also disbanded.

Independence

Some states, such as Estonia, Latvia, and Lithuania, declared themselves **independent,** while the others voluntarily joined together in a Commonwealth of Independent States in order to maintain their natural ties, while simultaneously maintaining their own independence.

This map shows the present-day Commonwealth of Independent States.

The new world

The fall of the Berlin Wall changed world history. The two halves of Germany—East and West—have been reunited. German politicians have had to face the difficult task of uniting the two parts while ensuring that the weakness of the old East German economy does not harm the prosperity that exists in West Germany. For the people attacking the Berlin Wall in November 1989, the fear of communism has gone, but there are new challenges for their country to face.

Across Eastern Europe, and in parts of Asia too, there are new issues to face. No longer does the mighty Soviet Union dominate the lives of the people. Now there are many independent countries striving to establish themselves. For them, the challenge is to develop their economies and systems of government to play a full part in international affairs. In Russia, people have greater political freedom, but there is widespread unemployment, high inflation, and a breakdown of law and order in many places.

The fall of the Berlin Wall proved to be a definite turning point in world history.

Important Dates

1917	November	**Communist** revolution in Russia
1939	August	Nazi-Soviet Pact signed
1941	June	Hitler invades **Soviet Union**
1946	March	Churchill makes his **Iron Curtain** speech
1947	March	Truman makes his **Truman Doctrine** speech
	June	**Marshall Plan** announced
1948	June	Berlin **blockade;** start of airlift
1949	April	Formation of NATO
1953	March	Death of Stalin
1955	May	Formation of Warsaw Pact
1956	November	Soviet tanks enter Hungary
1961	August	Construction of **Berlin Wall** begins
1962	October	Cuban missile crisis
1963	June	Kennedy makes *"Ich bin ein Berliner"* speech
1968		Beginning of Prague Spring
1972	May	SALT agreement signed
1973	January	Cease-fire agreed upon in Vietnam
1975		Communist troops overrun South Vietnam
	May	Helsinki Accords signed
1979	December	Soviet Union invades Afghanistan
1980	July	Moscow Olympics boycotted by United States
1985	March	Gorbachev becomes Soviet leader
1989	May	Breakup of Warsaw Pact begins
	November 9	Fall of Berlin Wall
	December	Bush and Gorbachev announce end of **Cold War**
1990	October 3	Germany reunited
	October 15	Gorbachev receives **Nobel Peace Prize**
1991	August	Attempted **coup** against Gorbachev; Communist party disbanded
	December 31	Soviet Union disbanded

Glossary

ally nation or state that is friendly to another nation

appeasement policy of trying to avoid war by negotiation and giving minor concessions

Berlin Wall fortified border built to divide East and West Berlin

blockade way of keeping goods or people from reaching a place

Bolshevik name of the political party later known as the Communist party

capitalism system that allows private ownership of land and industry, with the owners keeping the profits

capitalist person or state that follows capitalism

censorship forbidding newspapers and other media to print or say certain things

civil war war between people in the same country

Cold War time when countries are political enemies, but are not actually fighting each other in a full-scale war

communism system of government based on the idea that one ruling political party can run a country better than if ordinary people make their own decisions and keep private homes and businesses

communist person or state that follows communism

coup overthrowing of a government or its leader

czar name of the Russian head of state before the Revolution of 1917; sometimes shown as tsar

democracy system of government in which leaders are elected by the people

freedom of speech right to express a view without fear of punishment

guerrilla fighter who carries out ambushes and small-scale attacks

hot line telephone link between important heads of state

human right something that people should be able to have or do freely

independent not controlled by others

Iron Curtain expression describing how the democratic countries of Europe were separated from the communist ones after World War II

labor camp prison camp where people are forced to do long hours of hard physical work

Marshall Plan plan to give American economic aid to European countries after World War II to help them recover from the war

Nazi name used to describe Hitler's political party and brutal style of government in Germany; also a member of the party

Nobel Peace Prize prize awarded for making outstanding contributions to the welfare of humankind

propaganda twisting of information to portray a particular point of view

Soviet Union name of union of states in former Russia after the Revolution of 1917; also called the Union of Soviet Socialist Republics (USSR)

superpower name given to the U.S. and the Soviet Union after World War II

Truman Doctrine U.S. policy of helping countries resist communism

More Books to Read

Harvey, Miles. *The Fall of the Soviet Union.* Danbury, Conn.: Children's Press, 1995.

Mirable, Lisa. *The Berlin Wall.* Parsippany, N.J.: Silver Burdett Press, 1991.

Pietrusza, David. *The End of the Cold War.* San Diego, Calif.: Lucent Books, 1994.

Index